Who Are You?

NUMEROLOGY

Virginia Loh-Hagan

45TH PARALLEL PRESS

Published in the United States of America by Cherry Lake Publishing Group
Ann Arbor, Michigan
www.cherrylakepublishing.com

Reading Adviser: Marla Conn, MS, Ed., Literacy specialist, Read-Ability, Inc.
Book Designer: Felicia Macheske

Photo Credits: © Lapina/Shutterstock.com, cover; © donatas1205/Shutterstock.com, cover; © Lapina/Shutterstock.com, cover; © donatas1205/Shutterstock.com, cover; © Nomad_Soul/Shutterstock.com, 5; © cheapbooks/Shutterstock.com, 6; © Triff/Shutterstock.com, 9; © Bruce Rolff/Shutterstock.com, 11; © Kiselev Andrey Valerevich/Shutterstock.com, 12; © Dmytro Zinkevych/Shutterstock.com, 14; © ESB Professional/Shutterstock.com, 16; © blackboard1965/Shutterstock.com, 19; © sklyareek/Shutterstock.com, 20; © Krakenimages.com/Shutterstock.com, 23; © Olga Popova/Shutterstock.com, 25; © iordani/Shutterstock.com, 27; © Art_man/Shutterstock.com,29; © Byjeng/Shutterstock.com, 30

Graphics Throughout: © AKaiser/Shutterstock.com; © galastudio/Shutterstock.com; © tanyabosyk/Shutterstock.com; © ViSnezh/Shutterstock.com; © MARINA ARABADZHI/Shutterstock.com; © Alisa Burkovska/Shutterstock.com

45th Parallel Press is an imprint of Cherry Lake Publishing Group.

Library of Congress Cataloging-in-Publication Data

Names: Loh-Hagan, Virginia, author.
Title: Numerology / by Virginia Loh-Hagan.
Description: Ann Arbor, Michigan : Cherry Lake Publishing, 2020.
| Series: Who are you? | Includes index.
Identifiers: LCCN 2020006967 (print) | LCCN 2020006968 (ebook)
| ISBN 9781534169197 (hardcover) | ISBN 9781534170872 (paperback)
| ISBN 9781534172715 (pdf) | ISBN 9781534174559 (ebook)
Subjects: LCSH: Numerology—Juvenile literature.
Classification: LCC BF1623.P9 L59 2020 (print) | LCC BF1623.P9 (ebook) |
DDC 133.3/35—dc23
LC record available at https://lccn.loc.gov/2020006967
LC ebook record available at https://lccn.loc.gov/2020006968

Cherry Lake Publishing Group would like to acknowledge the work of the Partnership for 21st Century Learning, a Network of Battelle for Kids. Please visit *http://www.battelleforkids.org/networks/p21* for more information.

Printed in the United States of America
Corporate Graphics

Dr. Virginia Loh-Hagan is an author, university professor, and former classroom teacher. She was born on June 14, 1976. Her Life Path number is 7. She lives in San Diego, California, with her very tall husband and very naughty dogs. To learn more about her, visit www.virginialoh.com.

Chapter One

By the Numbers

What is numerology? What is a Life Path number? What are numerology portraits?

Numerology is a personality typing system. It uses numbers. It's a belief that numbers have meanings. It gives numerical values to letters, names, and ideas.

Numerologists are people who study numbers. They study number patterns. They interpret meanings. They think everything in the world is connected. They think everything is connected to numbers. They think nothing happens by accident. They think everything happens because of numbers. They think numbers have **vibrations**. Vibrations are special waves. They're like **vibes**, or energy.

Each number has a unique vibration. These vibrations shed light on people's personality traits. They describe people's actions. They give clues about people's futures. They tell people their lucky days.

There are different numerology systems. Learn more about them. Which one do you like the best?

The Life Path number is a person's most important number. It reveals a person's life purpose. It's based on a person's birthdate. It's found by adding all the numbers in the birthdate until it's a single **digit**. A digit is a number from 0 to 9.

Let's say Sloan's birthday is January 19, 2012.

1. Use the numerical form of the birthdate: 01/19/2012
2. Add the numbers together: 0 + 1 + 1 + 9 + 2 + 0 + 1 + 2 = 16
3. Add the numbers in the sum to get to one digit: 1 + 6 = 7

This means Sloan's Life Path number is 7.

When someone is aligned to their Life Path, they'll feel good. They'll feel balanced. When they act against their nature, they'll feel unbalanced.

Each month has a numerical value. For example, December is 12. What are the values of the other months?

FUN FACTS

* Numerology appears in the Harry Potter books. It was taught in the "Arithmancy" class at Hogwarts. Numbers were connected to words. They were used to predict the future. Studying numbers was Hermione Granger's favorite subject.

* Some people think 666 is evil. People think 666 means the devil. They think it means the end of the world. Hexakosioihexekontahexaphobia is the fear of 666.

* Shared birthdays can be explained mathematically by the "Birthday Problem." In a group of 23 people, there's a 50 percent chance that 2 people will have the same birthday.

* The number 23 is special. It's a prime number. Prime numbers are whole numbers that can't be divided by any number except for itself and 1. There are people called 23rdians. They believe 23 has magical powers. They see it everywhere. The number 23 shows up in history. Julius Caesar was stabbed 23 times.

Portraits are descriptions. Numerology portraits are also called numerology charts. They give a personalized guide to life. They reveal strengths. They reveal weaknesses. They reveal future selves. Numerologists create portraits using 6 numbers based on your name or birth date:

- **Life Path number:** This is a person's core identity.
- **Birthday number:** This reveals a person's special skills.
- **Attitude number:** This is how others see a person for the first time.
- **Soul Urge number:** This is a person's inner desires. It's what makes a person happy.
- **Personality number:** These are traits a person shows to others.
- **Power number:** This is a person's strengths.

Numbers can be used to reveal the hidden meanings of the world. What do you think are some of these hidden meanings?

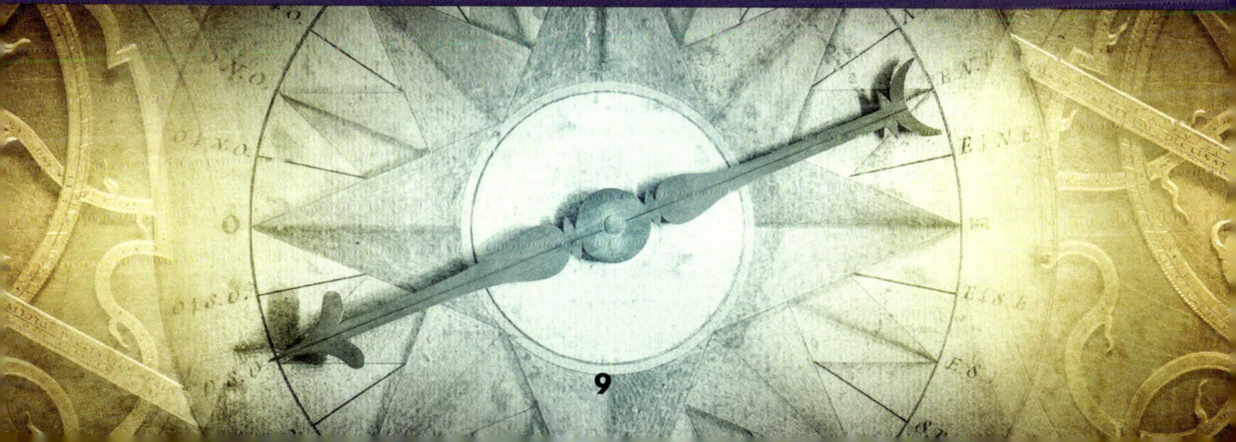

Chapter Two

Lucky Numbers

What are the personality types linked to each Life Path number? What are Master Numbers?

The Life Path numbers are connected to personality types.

Number 1 is the Leader. These types take action. They move things forward. They're **pioneers**. Pioneers are the first to do things. These types are independent. But they can be bossy. They can brag.

Number 2 is the Peacemaker. These types solve problems. They seek peace. They seek harmony. They care about the feelings of others. They're kind. They're sensitive. But they might cry too easily. They could be taken for granted.

Number 3 is the Talker. These types make good speeches. They argue well. They're creative. They invent things. They're artists. They inspire others. They make others happy. But their moods can quickly change.

Numerologists use this system to get meanings from names and words. They use it to get a person's **Destiny** number. Destiny means fate. This number shows how people will succeed in life.

Number 4 is the Teacher. These types are hard workers. They're responsible. They want to help others to grow and improve. They're builders. They like rules. But they can be stubborn.

Number 5 is the Free Spirit. These types are free thinkers. They like adventures. They're brave. They think about the future. They experience the world. They're playful. But they can be restless. They can be impatient.

Number 6 is the Giver. These types care for others. They nurture. They support. They protect their family and friends. They're healers. They're good with kids and animals. But they can be too controlling.

Read more about each Life Path. What are some areas of improvement for each number type?

Number 7 is the Seeker. These types are learners. They like to investigate. They're logical. They like details. They notice everything. They like things to be perfect. But they can be doubtful. They have a hard time making mistakes.

Number 8 is the Power Player. These types are successful. They have goals. They're charming. They like being the boss. But they can work too much. They can be selfish.

Number 9 is the Helper. These types serve the community. They think about the big picture. They are willing to make changes. But they can have short attention spans.

Helping your community is good for the soul. Do you do any community service?

EXPLAINED BY

SCIENCE

Dyscalculia is difficulty in learning math. People with this have a hard time understanding numbers. They have a hard time doing calculations. They have a hard time learning facts. They have a hard time telling time. They have a hard time measuring. About 5 to 10 percent of people have dyscalculia. About 11 percent of children with dyscalculia also have ADHD. ADHD is difficulty focusing. Dyscalculia looks different at different ages. It shows up more as children get older. It normally appears around ages 3 to 5. Dyscalculia can be genetic. This means people have it from birth. It runs in the family. Dyscalculia can be developed. This means people get it over time. Sometimes, people have brain injuries. This may cause difficulty in learning math. This is called acalculia. Brain studies have shown differences between people with and without dyscalculia. The brain is structured differently. Certain brain areas function differently.

Numerologists sometimes don't reduce sums of 11, 22, or 33. These are called Master Numbers. These numbers are super special.

Master Number 11 hypes up the energy of Number 2. These types heal themselves. They have high levels of awareness. They have strong gut feelings. They're good at reading people. Their senses are very strong. Nothing gets past them.

Master Number 22 hypes up the energy of Number 4. These types are master builders. They get things done. No task is too small for them.

Master Number 33 is the master of the master numbers. It hypes up the energy of Number 6. These types are very creative. They're also very passionate. Nothing stops them.

Some people think math is a "universal language." What do you think that means?

Chapter Three

Numbers over Time

Who is Pythagoras? What is Chaldean numerology? How did modern numerology develop?

Records of numerology appeared in many **ancient** cultures. Ancient means from a long time ago. Pythagoras was famous for his work in math and science. He's known as the Father of Numerology.

His work led to the Pythagorean number system. This system assigned letters to numerical values. This system uses a person's name and birthdate. A person's name number reveals the personality they show in public. A person's birthdate number reveals their life's purpose. Each number is reduced to a single digit.

However, there are Master Numbers. These are 11, 22, and 33. These often do not get reduced to a single digit.

Pythagoras is famous for the Pythagorean theorem. The equation is $a^2 + b^2 = c^2$. Can you name some other equations?

Spell out your first and last name. What number did you get? For example, Maya Lin's power number would be 3:

Maya: 4 + 1 + 7 + 1 = **13**

Lin: 3 + 9 + 5 = **17**

13 + 17 = **30**

3 + 0 = **3**

1 = A, J, S	**4 = D, M, V**	**7 = G, P, Y**
2 = B, K, T	**5 = E, N, W**	**8 = H, Q, Z**
3 = C, L, U	**6 = F, O, X**	**9 = I, R**

Pythagoras connected math to musical notes. Do you see how math and music are connected?

REAL-LIFE CONNECTION

Chinese people have their own numerology system. They believe in lucky numbers. Certain numbers are luckier than others. For example, 8 is very lucky. It rhymes with the Chinese word for "fortune." But 4 is very unlucky. The number 4 sounds like the Chinese word for "death." Chinese people avoid buying houses with the number 4. They fear bad things happening. There's an apartment building in Long Island City, New York. It doesn't have a fourth floor. Builders wanted it to be lucky according to Chinese customs. Lucky numbers come in pairs. Lucky number combinations are 99 and 888. The number 99 means eternal. Eternal means lasting forever. The number 888 means triple fortune. It means "rich, rich, rich." Chinese people are willing to pay a lot for lucky numbers. The telephone number 8888-8888 was sold for $270,723 in Chengdu, China. Realtors price homes at $888,888. In 2008, the Beijing Olympics opened on 08/08/08 at 08:08:08 p.m.

Pythagoras traveled. He went to Egypt. He was inspired by **Chaldean** numerology. Chaldean refers to ancient Iraq. This system mostly uses a person's name. The first name reveals how a person's energy and personality are shown in public and social settings. The middle name reveals a person's desires and hidden talents. The last name reveals how a person is influenced by their family. Similar to the Pythagorean number system, this system also reduces the number to a single digit, except for the Master Numbers (11, 22, and 33).

1 = A, Q, Y, I, J	4 = D, M, T	7 = O, Z
2 = B, R, K	5 = E, H, N, X	8 = F, P
3 = G, C, L, S	6 = U, V, W	

What are the three numbers from your first, middle, and last names?

Mrs. L. Dow Balliett lived from 1847 to 1929. She studied Pythagoras's work. She helped create modern numerology. She wrote books. She spoke at events. She connected numbers to people. She connected numbers to colors.

Other numerologists continued to develop the system. They connected numbers to personalities. They connected numbers to events.

Some people don't believe in numerology. They think it's a fake science. What do you think?

Chapter Four

Famous Examples

Who is Frida Kahlo? Who is Marie Curie? Who is Jackie Kennedy Onassis?

Frida Kahlo was born on July 6, 1907. Her Life Path number is 3. This makes sense. Kahlo is thought to be Mexico's greatest artist. Kahlo was a painter. She painted many pictures of herself. She used bright colors.

Kahlo was very inspirational. At age 6, she got polio. She was in bed for 9 months. Polio damaged her left leg and foot. Kahlo walked with a limp. At age 18, she was in a bus accident. She was hurt very badly. A steel rod went through her hip. But she never quit. She kept making art. She became a hero for many women.

Who are your favorite artists?
Find out their Life Path numbers.

Marie Curie was born on November 7, 1867. Her Life Path number is 4. This makes sense. Curie was a hard worker. She was a scientist. Her discoveries changed science. Many scientists learned from her. She studied rays. She discovered 2 elements. She helped develop **X-rays**. X-rays are special energy. They can be used to take pictures inside bodies. Curie helped during World War I. She invented special X-ray machines. The machines could be moved to soldiers hurt on battlefields. Curie won 2 Nobel Prizes. She is the only woman to win it twice. She gave away a lot of her money. Her work saved many lives.

Figure out the Life Path numbers of your family and friends. Do they match their descriptions?

SPOTLIGHT

BIOGRAPHY

George Lucas was born on May 14, 1944. His Life Path number is 1. He's a famous movie director. He's famous for the Indiana Jones movies. He's famous for the Star Wars movies. His lucky number is 1138. These numbers are from his college telephone number. He went to the University of Southern California. He studied films. His first movie was *THX 1138*. It was made in 1971. It's science fiction. It's about a future controlled by machines. The number 1138 appears in a lot of Lucas's movies. It also appears in Lucas's media projects. He has TV shows. He has video games. He has books. In *Star Wars: A New Hope*, Chewbacca is sent to cell block 1138. In *Star Wars: The Force Awakens*, a stormtrooper is called 1138. In several Star Wars movies, 1138 is written on helmets. In *Indiana Jones and the Kingdom of the Crystal Skull*, THX-1138 was on a car license plate.

Jackie Kennedy Onassis was born on July 28, 1929. Her Life Path number is 11. This makes sense. Onassis was married to President John F. Kennedy. She was First Lady of the United States. She was also married to Aristotle Onassis. He was one of the richest men in the world.

Onassis was very influential. She was known for her style. She was in touch with the people. She restored the White House. She opened the White House to the public. She started a kindergarten in the White House. She spoke several languages. She helped build friendships with world leaders. She worked as a book editor.

Look around. Pay attention to what's going on around you. What number patterns do you see?

WHO ARE YOU?

TAKE THE QUIZ!

What are some ideal jobs for you? Some people think Life Path numbers are connected to work.

1 Business Owner, Director, Editor

2 Architect, Chef, Judge

3 Artist, Athlete, Inventor

4 Accountant, Computer Programmer, Engineer

5 Actor, Lawyer, Salesperson

6 Musician, Nurse, Teacher

7 Author, Counselor, Photographer

8 Banker, Coach, Realtor

9 Civil Rights Leader, Politician, Scientist

What is your lucky gemstone? Numerology states gems can affect people's moods.

1 Ruby

2 Pearl

3 Yellow sapphire

4 Garnet

5 Emerald

6 Diamond

7 Cat's eye (chrysoberyl)

8 Blue sapphire

9 Coral

DISCLAIMER: All the quizzes and questions in this book are designed for entertainment purposes only. They shouldn't be used as advice. They shouldn't be taken seriously. There is no guarantee of accuracy. They are not valid or reliable. But they're fun! To download a copy of this quiz, please visit: https://cherrylakepublishing.com/teaching_guides.

Where should you live? There are certain places that would fit your Life Path number's personality type.

1 **You should live in a major city.** An example is Los Angeles, California.

2 **You should live abroad. Abroad means being in a foreign country.** An example is Paris, France.

3 **You should live in an urban setting. Urban means city.** An example is Phoenix, Arizona.

4 **You should live in a suburban setting. Suburban means outside the city.** An example is Fairfax, Virginia.

5 **You should live on an island.** An example is Whidbey Island, Washington.

6 **You should live in a small town.** An example is Taos, New Mexico.

7 **You should live in a college town.** An example is Ann Arbor, Michigan.

8 **You should live in a capital city.** An example is Washington, D.C.

9 **You should travel to different cities.** An example is to help build houses in various cities.

Which superhero embodies your Life Path number? Superheroes have personality traits too!

1 **Black Panther**

2 **Captain Marvel**

3 **Black Widow**

4 **Hulk**

5 **Thor**

6 **Captain America**

7 **Doctor Strange**

8 **Iron Man**

9 **Spiderman**

Glossary

ancient (AYN-shuhnt) from a time long ago

Chaldean (KAL-dee-uhn) relating to ancient Iraq

destiny (DES-tuh-nee) fate

digit (DIJ-it) a single number from 0 to 9

numerologists (noo-mur-AH-luh-jists) professionals who practice numerology

numerology (noo-mur-AH-luh-jee) a personality typing system based on numbers

pioneers (pye-uh-NEERZ) trailblazers, people who are the first to do something

portraits (POR-trits) descriptions or overviews

vibes (VIBEZ) energy

vibrations (vye-BRAY-shuhnz) special waves

X-rays (EKS-rayz) special energy that can pass through solid things

Index